To Tony B

African Talk

Enjoy

May God continue to
bless you!
Sincerely
yours

African Talk

Carlos Vintes Pender

VANTAGE PRESS
New York

Cover art by Okuku

FIRST EDITION

Copyright © 2002 by Carlos Vintes Pender

Published by Vantage Press, Inc.
516 West 34th Street, New York, New York 10001

Manufactured in the United States of America
ISBN: 0-533-13783-7

Library of Congress Catalog Card No.: 00-093264

0 9 8 7 6 5 4 3 2 1

To Pernolia Vintes Martin and all the Heavenly Blessings from being your son.

With a special thank you to Barbara Williamson, retired city of Cleveland school teacher; without your help this book would not have been published.

A special thanks to Mrs. Lizabeth Okuku Bombata for the use of Prince Emmanuel Okuku's exceptional artwork.

Special thanks as well to Dunstan L. Haettenschwiller for permission to reprint the artwork of his late wife, Evelyn Davis Haettenschwiller. In loving memory of a great friend in Christ.

Contents

Introduction

As we head into the new millennium, it is time to **renew old words of wisdom**. The laws of knowledge, like wealth, are extended for the good use of all. The laws of use are universal, and he who violates them suffers by reason of his conflict with all God's natural orderly forces.

Why study this book? What is the African connection to America? What is the African connection to the Bible? What is the African connection to our future?

African Talk reveals a human society where the total community takes care of its problems, a society in which the hungry are fed, the sick are cared for, and the old are cherished. The old African societies had a built-in social security system; we should look to them as models and apply God's good ideas as we usher in the twenty-first century.

I hope that *African Talk* will ignite a new brotherhood among all people of every race toward the realization that we are all here together. The time is now for a resounding truth, the truth found in *African Talk*.

Abortion

Has the thought of you being aborted ever disturbed you?

Where there is no male influence, the offspring suffers.

It would be considered sacrilegious if a man could conceive and have an abortion.

I knew you before you were born.

For those of us who cannot protect ourselves, we are all responsible.

Silence, more silence, and more silence.
A journey's end.

Absence

All hearts forget a little during absence.

Ajuba Mother and Twins

Accomplishment

Your deeds will always be remembered when you forget what
you have done for others.

If no one cares who gets the credit, anything can be
accomplished.

Most men will never do great things, but we can
all do small things in a great way.

Achievement

Success is the sole judge of who is the best hunter.

It is always better to be better than you think you can
be.

Some people are so poor, they can't pay attention.

Three Atitagu sisters

Advice

One must listen more and talk less.

People fail to remember that families are forever.

The road to a friend's house is never lined with thorn
bushes.

The words that fall off a drunk man's tongue, are the
same
words on a sober man's mind.

Africa

Yesterday Africa was your father.

African truths can never be told so as to be understood
and not be believed.

Africa exports truth almost the way
Greece exports myths.

When African talk is told to a fool, its meaning
has to be explained to him.

African talk is the daughter of truth and the son of love.

Where on earth is the Alpha and Omega, the Level and
the Plumb, O latitude and O longitude? Africa!

The world fell in love with Egypt.

If you don't respect Africa, the jackals will sing
over your grave.
The wild beast catches you on the path you do not fear.

Witches and witch doctors ride the night on the sloping
backs of hyenas.

God made me part African, not an African African but a new
admixture American African.

Jesus Christ's first view of the world was that of
the pyramids and the Sphinx.

The longest kiss is when the Blue
Nile and the White Nile meet.

Young Winabi Girl

Agreement

The way to know if a man is learned is if his views
coincide with yours.

When you get even, you are not getting ahead.

Ambition

A man with too much ambition never sleeps in peace.

He who commands patience can have what he wills.

Animals

All animals and all people of the same kind
love to look at each other.

Animals don't care about age,
they welcome each other as young as they feel.

For a bird to fly, he must use both wings.

Two eagles disputed about a fish, when a kite
swooped down and carried it off.

The monkey enters the hut when the man is away
and eats up the maize.

When the panther is away, his cubs are also eaten.

The monkey one day cuts his own throat,
all the time copying everybody.

A fool will pair an ox with a boar.

When the bee visits your house, let him be; you may
want to
visit the bee's house one day.

The boar wanted to be as big as the elephant—he burst.

An ant may even harm an elephant.

The eagle, because he soars high next to God's roof,
must see what God sees.

The Egyptian female eagle is larger than the male: she kills
larger prey; he kills the smaller prey.

A cockroach never wins his case in a court of fowls.

The bleeding heart monkey also resides in Africa.

Although a water sign, scorpions can't swim, they drown in
rain water.

Why are there no pictures of camels on the pyramids' walls?

The cockroach and the scorpion as in ancient times
are still with us.

The honey badger and the goshawk are married forever
but they never build a nest.

Ancestors

When we are awake and when we are asleep, the spirits of
our fathers walk the earth unseen.

Look to your village to find your history. Look to your father to
find your spirit.

Anticipation

When love in the heart overflows, it comes out through the mouth.

In times of great need, your friends measure themselves.

Do not make garments for the baby before it is born.

Appearance

Because he's seen first, a tall man must dress better
than a short man.

Nothing does more harm than a cunning man
who passes for a wise man.

Among so many millions what a wonder that there
should be no two faces alike.

The most beautiful fruit may contain a worm.

Appreciation

Works of art that are most cherished
are works done least rapidly.

A woman who receives a gift does not measure it.

The greatest source of information we have about the
past and the future comes from Egypt.

New Dimensions

Art

The artist who has feelings for the complete woman
is a saved man.

A change in civilizations leads to a change in art.

To the heavenly paintbrush that made creatures' colors,
stripes
and spots, we are forever thankful.

The Egyptians have a lock on hair styles and makeup.

Why are there no pictures of camels on the pyramid
walls?

Aspirations

What one has is always less than what one hopes for.

Lonely men sit beside each other and pray for wisdom to
remember their courage.

Passion is a hard thing
to conceal.

Associates

The distance one should keep from an evil man
cannot be measured.

Flee from the friend who associates with your enemies.

Attitude

A man is bad tempered when he is wrong.

The light in a woman's eyes will undo a man's heart.

A woman's silence stirs a man
and excites his subconscious mind.

Some girls have class that's never been used.

Bad Advice

Unfaithfulness in marriage calms the woman
and excites the man.

Barren

A woman without a good man is like a flower with no
seeds.

Oba Louie

Beginnings

To a young child, God and his creations appear exciting.

God always rewards righteousness
with plenty.

Betterment

Wealth is a good handmaiden but a bad mistress.

Brotherhood

Your shoulder is for your brother.

A strong man needs few male partners.

Make those near you happy, and those who are far away
will
come nearer.

He who is great among us must be our servant.

Brave

A brave man is one who admits he fears God.

The currency of war is blood, don't invest yours;
spend your enemies.

It's not too late to be brave tomorrow.

Fear of fear and the dread of fear shape the heart of a
brave man.

In war, valor makes a man immortal.

A warrior who isn't afraid to walk in dark places
is afraid of no man.

Buildings

If a tool breaks while building a house, do you stop
building or do you change the tool?

Burden

If you do things you should not do, you must bear
what you could not bear.

If you don't use your head, your feet
will have to pay.

A newborn baby is both a joy and a burden.

Caution

He who has been bitten by a snake fears a lizard.

Never say the first thing that comes to your mind.

Change

Failure to change is a universal sin.

The locusts swarm, the year changes.

If you refuse to be made straight when young, you will
not be
made straight when you are old.

Ajuba Mother and Child

Character

Those who are absent are always wrong, until they
return.

Only a baboon understands a baboon.

Children

Advise and counsel your son; if he does not listen,
let adversity be his teacher.

If your son laughs when you scold him, you ought to cry,
for
you have lost him; if he cries you may laugh,
for you have a worthy heir.

It is not the duty of elders to wait on children,
but for children to wait on elders.

Correct your children before they correct you.

If you despise a child, you cannot teach him.

A woman should never hide the father from the child.

All children want to be
disciplined, if you don't discipline
them they feel unloved.

A disrespectful and disobedient son is no son at all.

Ikot Bride and Groom

Civilized

The last thing civilized by man will be woman.

Commandment

God commands us to serve or suffer.

A man must let his brain lie with a woman who his
heart lies with also.

In all times, in all places, the truth is beautiful.

Common Sense

No matter how shiny the bracelet, if it fits you wear it,
but if
it hurts you throw it away.

There are a million kinds of fool killers, but only one
kind of common sense.

If you climb up a tree, to get down you must
climb down that same tree.

If you depend on forces outside of yourself, you will be
dominated by them.

Communication

A fool talks and talks, a wise man listens.

If a man tells you something three times, it is true.

No man tells all he knows.

Being told is different from being seen.

If you think of something you should not say, roll it over
your
tongue one time and swallow.

If a friend demands your silence, he is not your friend.

Companions

A monkey does not see his own hind parts;
he sees his neighbor's.

The owl and the bat belong to another realm of the
imagination.

A rich man and a poor man never play together.

West African Dancers

Complacency

Contentment with what you have achieved kills progress.

The aggressive animal (man) gets more to eat, has a better chance to mate, keeps its offspring safer and leaves more descendants.

Constant Presence

The cockroach and the scorpion as in ancient times are still with us.

No matter where you go, there you are.

Conversation

Loving one another is talking with one another.

A fool thinks he is being praised when he is being cursed.

Convictions

A fault confessed is half redressed.

If you are rich, you are hated; if you are poor,
you are despised.

African truths will never hurt the teller.

Cooperation

When two spider webs unite, they can tie up
the largest insect.

A good business partner will not add obstacles to it.

Courage

A warrior is the little boy who grew up to be like his
father.

Share your courage with others, but keep
your fears to yourself.

Men don't follow titles, they follow courage.

The bride of courage is faith.

Muas Witch Doctor

Cowardice

A man full of precautions is a coward.

Is there a heaven for cowards?

The penalty for assassination is disembowelment.

A coward will sweat in cold water.

An insecure religion breeds cowards.

Cowards have no morals, no remorse, no compassion, no future.

Cycle

Nature is the artwork of God, and all things are artificial.

The circumference of the pyramid is equal to pi—3.141590265.

Wait until you die, before you're dead.

Danger

A lion roaring kills no one.

The adult male oryx will defend an unrelated young oryx.

Daring

When the turtle crosses a road, he too must stick his
head out.

Day

In the sunset we see all the vast colors, where the day
joins
past eternities.

Men think about women on two occasions, day and
night.

A man who is wrong early in the morning is wrong all
day.

The sunset divides the sky; the moon is up,
yet it is not night.

Deceit

Never leave your host's house throwing mud in his well.

Carrying a bag of grain with a hole in it is the same as
confiding
a secret to an unworthy friend.

The Beggar

Decisions

A hen will find a corner to lay in,
however full the henhouse.

If you choose to choose time, you save time.

Moses did not take a poll when he left Egypt.

The crocodiles decision to bite is no decision at all.

Despair

To love a woman who does not love you is like shaking
dew drops from a tree after a long, hot day.

Failure, like divorce, is shrouded in excuses.

The hard woman loses her man to the soft woman.

Determination

A woman seldom asks advice before she makes
her wedding dress.

It's the wandering dog that finds the old bone.

If no family member heeds your call, go forth alone.

Development

If a small tree grows in the shade of a larger tree,
it will die small.

Those who achieve adulthood enjoy a throne others
have yet to reach.

Devotion

A baby and love must be treated tenderly.

Difference

To do work the knee can be bent, but the heart
cannot be bent for love.

Every wave has its own integrity.

Hearts and souls are colorless.

Ikot Fisherman

Disagreement

Children of the same parents do not always agree.

Different children from different fathers in one home seldom agree.

Discontent

Why are the rich always complaining?

Divinity

A beautiful woman is proof that God loves us.

What separates Jesus from others is that he descended and ascended.

Dreams

The cousin to death is sleep.

It is good to dream in color.

Earth

The queen of beds is the earth.

The universal sign for earth is the cross.

Where on Earth is the Alpha and Omega, the Level and
the Plumb, O latitude O longitude? Africa.

Eating

A bird flies high in search for food but always
lands to feed.

In the air, in water, or on the earth, the top predators
dine alone.

Education

Education makes man easy to lead, difficult to push,
easy to
govern, and impossible to enslave.

Of all the creatures on earth, humans require
the longest education.

A fool sees not the same tree as the educated man sees.

The baby jackal gets the best of both worlds, it is
educated by both the mother and the father.

Enjoyment

Laughter shows in one or two spots, although you feel good
sensations all over.

Ensnare

Women ambush men in the cradle, in the kitchen,
and in the bedroom.

Envy

Why do you hurt when your friend succeeds?

The easiest form of mental activity is criticism; the
toughest is creativity.

Ethics

Is the man who uses the spear more savage than the man
who uses the cannon?

Togo Spirits

Evil

Evil enters the brain like a needle and spreads
like a grapevine.

Expect evil, if you have done evil.

Evil ways know where evil sleeps.

Evolution

All things are destroyed by time.

Example

Do not be like the flea and bite the owner of the house.

A child says what he has heard at home.

If a bird looks good, it flies good.

Excess

He who hunts more than one rat catches none.

Experience

He who has learned his lessons well teaches others.

A man who makes no mistakes, never makes anything.

Yambo Queens

Fact

If wisdom says one thing, nature will never say another.

The jungle is beautiful but unjust and unfit for the
weak.

Man's wisdom has limitations, but God
put no limit on stupidity.

The man who will not shave you does not cut you.

He who has seen with his own eyes, let him speak.

Slaves feel hunger, and kings feel hunger.

A horse falls, yet he has four legs.

Raindrops beat upon the zebra's skin, but rain does
not wash away his stripes.

No one crosses a river without getting wet.

All good things have a foundation of good order.

It is the little things that are symbolic.

Pharaoh threw a written message into the Nile to order
it to rise.

The sweetest milk is in the cow.

Without the sun, the moon
would be a dark circle.

Facetious Advice

To catch more women, chase them downhill.

Family

Dine with strangers but save your love for the family.

Affairs of the home are not talked about
on the public square.

A negative family member puts a burden on the whole
family.

Your shoulder is for your brother.

Fate

An evil or stupid son cannot be chosen by the Father.

What was God's fate for my aborted son?

The key to failure in life is trying to please everybody.

Kummu King and Queen

Father

From our fathers we get our names;
from our virtues we get our honor.

The older I get, the wiser my father becomes.

Fatherly Advice

If you know a man's friends, you know the man.

For a better tomorrow, give daily.

A woman or man who deliberates too much is lost.

A place worth going has no shortcuts.

Faults

To be conscious of no faults is the greatest of all faults.

Feelings

Sometimes, especially among women, revenge is sweet.

Fools

It is better to be in prison with a wise man
than to be in paradise with a fool.

The fool killer will claim and destroy any man who
continues to go out of his element.

A fool's heart is in his mouth, but a wise man's
mouth is in his heart.

Everyone dies a death that befits his character.

Not to know is bad, but not to wish to know is worse.

Luck may visit a fool, but luck never sits down with
him.

It is better to close your mouth and be thought a fool,
than to open your mouth and be known a fool.

Foolishness

To be intimate with a foolish friend is like going
to bed with a razor.

Do not tell the man who is carrying you that he stinks.

Only a fool tries to jump fire.

A man does not call to his dog with a whip in his hand.

A person who hides his disease cannot expect to find a
cure.

After our long, hard struggle
why act like a buffoon?

Fortitude

To try and to fail is not laziness.

Zaire Girls

Foul Words

An ear that is healthy can stand hearing sick foul words.

If the foul words from your mouth turned into a knife, they would cut off your lips.

Freedom

Men who never benefit from their own work become lazy.

Friends

To be poor indeed is to be without a friend.

Our friends' friends are our friends.

Friendship is like a bank vault; you can't continue to draw out from it without making any deposits.

Friction

Gunpowder and fire do not sleep together.

If you despise a child you
cannot teach him.

Generosity

The measurement of a man's mind is the shade
it casts on others.

God

Just when we think God is far off, He comes close to us.

To Jesus Christ, the pyramids represented both a
solar symbol and social symbol.

I knew you before you were born.

When you make a promise to God, you must give up
something you don't need.

The Sacred Heart Jesus

God's Abundance

All stars have crosses in the middle.

Rain means life.

God's Commandments

The knowledge of some supreme divine power
keeps men in order.

Let love be genuine.

Go in peace.

The law of knowledge like wealth is extended for the
good use for all.

God's Creations

All God's gifts put man's best dreams to shame.

Night by night we look right through the heavens above
and see God's roof.

Stars are like God's teeth, they sparkle like the
underbelly of a fish.

The bleeding heart monkey also lives in Africa.

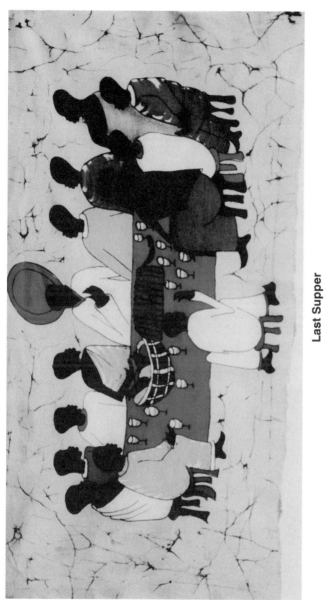

Last Supper

God's Gifts

Children are the supreme gifts from God.

God does not want to change the past.

He who knows God and knows that he knows God
is a rich, wise man.

God's Goodness

The hand that made us is divine.

God made the body to transport the brain.

God's Knowledge

The nature of God is a circle of which the center is
everywhere.

Fruit that falls without shaking the tree is too soft to
eat.

Jesus Christ's first long view of the world was that of
the pyramids and the Sphinx.

Good Advice

If you don't stand for something, you will fall for anything.

Before shooting the bow, one must aim.

To be loved is better than to be feared.

It is better to travel alone than with a bad companion.

When walking up the mountain, lead with your good leg. When coming down, lead with your bad leg.

Gossip

A person who talks incessantly talks nonsense.

Gratitude

If a man and a woman give mutual affection, each gets his share.

The Gossipers

Greatness

In Africa you can see more and look farther than any place in the world.

The beauty of God is like unto water in the sun.

Whatever I have coming, it's not up to you.

No civilization has used time to the same degree of measurement as the Egyptians.

Anybody can be great, anybody can serve.

Growth

A river still wants to grow, no matter how full it gets.

Bananas grow little by little.

Never think that you will not live to grow old.

Guilt

Remorse always comes after a foolish deed.

When you do not give mutual gifts, friendships
are not cemented.

Habit

After the rat has passed, then you set the trap.

Happiness

When we are happy, love's all right and things are
changing.

Make those near you happy, and those who are far
away will come nearer.

Happiness does not produce
gratitude, gratitude produces
happiness.

Harmony

The fall of a nation begins in the homes of its people.

Heart

The knee can bend, but
the heart cannot bend.

A fool's heart is in his
mouth, but a wise man's
mouth is in his heart.

Help

In traveling, someone else's legs do you no good.

Hiding

If you are hiding on the mountain or in the valley,
do not light a fire.

When hunting do not bathe.

Mary

Holding

When you hold a man down, you must also stay down with him.

Honesty

To work for profit is no shame.

Hope and Truth

Sunlight is private property to a man in prison.

A crooked river grants each traveler new hope.

There is nothing without life.

Things really do work out in the end.

As long as you are standing on the dirt and not the dirt standing on you, you have a chance.

Human Nature

Some women are like a river—beautiful but crooked.

Humility

A man may be in possession of the truth and yet
be forced to surrender.

Husband

A husband should never let the sun rise on an angry
wife.

Ideas

Throughout history, historians have decided that Jesus
Christ fit
into all man's aspirations.

Idealism

The weed that grows in every man's soul is slavery.

For Americans in the New Millennium, we either hang
close together or we hang separately.

Ignorance

Ignorance is more expensive than any education.

Ignorance is a steep hill with perilous rocks at the bottom.

Immaturity

A daughter who is silly tries to teach her mother how to bear children.

Immoral

The rule among thieves is that nothing is too large or too small to steal.

Immortality

A man who is fault free will never die.

Impossibility

Do not dispose of the lion's claw before he is dead.

Benin Shrine

Inactivity

In one's old age, it's easy to become a monk.

Individuality

What is good luck for one man is bad luck for another.

If your mother were an onion and your father were a garlic, who could be offended by you?

Ingratitude

One recovers from a sickness but forgets about God's cure afterwards.

Instinct

Music makes you move your neck.

Integrity

Men who love in haste detest at leisure.

Intelligence

A man with common sense has all the sense he needs.

The complexion of the mind and the complexion of the skin are two different things.

Involvement

Playing a part in life is better than playing apart.

Every town furnishes its own women.

Job

In every trade, a man must serve his time.

The Drum Announcers

Joy

What a joy! The joy of victory.

Joy and pain are followed by sunshine and rain.

People will try to steal your joy, if you let them.

The laughter of a baby is a delight to the soul.

Judging

Never judge a man by the way he looks.

Knowledge

Knowledge grows by taking things apart; wisdom grows
by
putting things together.

Like a garden, knowledge if not cultivated cannot
be harvested.

A man who does not know one thing knows another.

Laziness

To sit all day is to be crippled.

Life

Why is the long life the best life?

When we cannot reach what we love, we love what is within
our reach.

The man sitting down loses his share to the man on his feet.

There is a rhythm to life, we sleep at night and wake up in the morning.

As long as you are standing on dirt and the dirt is not standing on you, you have a chance.

Like

A cobra snake does not bite another cobra snake.

Likable

To stay alive in all the hearts we leave behind is not to
die ever.

Limitations

A wise man will make more opportunities than he finds.

Little Things

A third of a loaf is better than no bread.

When a man and a woman
give mutual affection each
gets their share.

Loneliness

A man in a home without a woman is like
a barn without cattle.

Lonely men sit beside each
other and pray for wisdom
to remember their courage.

Fu Fu Family

Love

Christ died not just for the men he knew and loved,
but all mankind.

A cliff becomes a waterfall when one is in love.

Love is likened to a misty rain, coming slowly, but
flooding the heart's rivers.

The palace in the heart is the dome of love.

My soul got caught up in love and was taught
a whole new rhythm.

Happiness can be thought, caught, and taught, but
never bought.

The nature of life is only love, and love is only bliss.

Hatred has no medicine to cure it, except love.

Let love be genuine.

Love's alright and things are changing.

When love in the heart overflows, it comes out through
the mouth.

Some things come, some things go, but Romanticism
will always be.

Is there not one thing in your life worth losing
everything for?

Luck

Luck may visit a fool, but luck never sits down with
him.

Only after you have crossed the river can you say the
crocodile was not hungry.

Malice

A word uttered can never be taken back.

Although quarrels end, words once spoken never die.

To hate and be violent is demeaning to God.

Udooh Musical Troop

Man

Man is like berry wine. When young, sweet but without strength. In old age, strong—less sweet—but potent.

All the world admires a man with deep affection.

A rich man and a poor man can never play together.

A wise man can conceal from others what he does not know.

A man is happy when he finds a woman who adds quality to his life.

A man who plants trees loves many others besides himself.

A man who boasts of sin is a devil; he who falls into sin is a
man; and he who grieves at sin is a saint.

What man knows a man better than his wife?

A man full of precaution is a coward.

What man can live by profit alone?

Man/Woman

To kiss for the first time you only get one chance.

Marriage

God will not change marriage!

Maturity

Some men learn late in life to say "I don't know."

We acquire knowledge too slowly and age too fast.

Mercy

Because animals are not evil, it's easy for man
to show mercy.

Middle Ages

The greatest man-made monument is in Africa.

Cape Fisherman

Misfortune

If bread is the staff of life, why do so many eat crumbs?

Whether the sword falls on the man or the man on the
sword, the man suffers.

Victory in the jungle is avoiding disaster.

Morality

Vice itself lost half its evil, by losing all its grossness.

Our souls get caught up in love, and are taught
a whole new rhythm.

By nature, man is either a beast or a god.

Nature

In Africa, all rain means life.

Of all the responsibilities the sun has in the universe,
as if it had nothing more to do, it ripens fruit.

Nature is the art of God, and all things are artificial.

All things that come to perfection will soon
perish with time.

The moon crosses the mountain slowly.

The head must grow first, before horns can grow.

The leopard plays with the captured jackal; it allows it
to run
off and almost escape again and again the way a
cat plays with a mouse.

Obedience

Follow all customs or flee the country.

Obstacles

Words of no importance stop great events.

Opinion

High failure in life is overlapped by low success.

Seeing is greater than hearing.

Opportunity

First you see opportunity, then it will face you. Be prepared to meet it.

When God sends opportunity, he who is asleep does not wake up.

Optimism

Enjoy good by anticipating good.

Masi Hunter and Wife

Order

Things are two and two in all the world.

Like the days of the week, events follow each other.

The rainbow is the unstrung bond with God.

The first plant to respond to water is the desert hyssop.

Past

Nothing moves in this world that is not African
in its origin.

Past civilizations are human volcanoes, burned out.

All things are destroyed by time.

Like the sun, African truths never grow old.

Listen to the wind and hear the voices of your life.

Perception

Like Africa, people are more attractive up close.

It is not the loss of men that makes a nation extinct,
but the loss of women.

If your subliminal mind says go see a friend, go!

Deception increases stress.

A prophet's mission is not chosen, yet he risks his life.

The pharaoh's mouth is left open for a dribble of semen
from the stars.

Planning

Always plan more than you can do, then do it.

Trips are not spoiled by making preparations.

The time to start preparations is not the day
on which you start out.

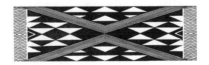

Praying Hands

Positive Thinking

If there is a hole nearby, the mouse laughs at the cat.

Things aren't the best things in life.

Most of the things we worry about never happen.

Poverty

Three kinds of people die poor: those who move around too much, those who incur debts, and those who divorce.

You can lose wealth faster than you can gain it.

Prayer

Night by night we look right through the heavens above
and
see God's roof.

Pray that your country is right, but right or wrong,
pray for your country.

Price

All cures have a cost.

The penalty for assassination is disembowelment.

Pride

A man who is too modest goes hungry.

After our long hard struggles, why act like a buffoon?

Probation

Your wife is on trial each time you sit down to eat her food.

Profanity

The taste of foul words each day will inevitably make you dumb.

The neighbor who entered your house cursing is not a Christian.

If the foul words from your mouth turned into a knife they would cut off your lips.

Wedding Offering

Progress

The truth can never be told so as to be understood
and not be believed.

Protection

A wise shepherd does not strike his flock.

Prosperity

It's bad to give an evil person prosperity.

Some people are so poor they can't pay attention.

Quarrel

It takes two people to make a quarrel.

Underwater Dreams

Reality

A broken jar is worse than spilled water.

If a toothache were in the foot, one would be lame.

No medicine can save a dying man.

Like soap, if you try to cleanse too many others,
you will waste away.

Rain never falls on one roof alone.

No one crosses a river without getting wet.

The rice that is sweet is eaten quickly.

A nation that does not have a cure for an illness
(disease)
must learn to live with it.

Darkness conceals even the elephant.

Slavery is poverty.

Rebellious

It is a bad child who refuses good advice from his elders.

All children want to be disciplined, if you don't
discipline them they feel unloved.

Recovery

You may recover from a slip of the foot, but from a slip of the
tongue you may never recover.

Regret

A man who marries a very beautiful woman marries
·   trouble.

There is always a hidden
treasure lost in a vanquished
people.

Relationships

A man with wealth wins many women.

Respect

The older I get, the wiser my father becomes.

Calling Nature

Retribution

The fear of some supreme divine power keeps men in
order.

Revenge

If a man injured your pig, do not go out and kill his bull.

Let go, let God.

Rhythm

He who has no dance rhythm will say the drum
is out of tune.

My soul got caught up in love and was taught a whole
new rhythm.

There is a rhythm to life, we sleep at night and wake up
in the morning.

Rich

He who knows God and knows that he knows God
is a rich, wise man.

West African Musical Troupe

Risk

When a Nubian warrior tells you not to cross his land,
and
you don't stop, that's suicide.

Sadness

If the heart is sad, few words come out of the mouth.

To love a woman who does not love you is like shaking
dewdrops from a tree after a long hot day.

Satisfaction

Oh, what a joy, the joy of victory.

Science

Man does not know where heaven starts or stops.

The heaven is made perfect around, but the earth is
made with
broken arcs.

A woman should be embraced close with the right hand
and
pushed away with the left hand.

Built on the 30th parallel North, the Great Pyramids
face the
constellation Orion. Perfectly N.S.E.W.

Secret

Do not hide the father of the child from the child.

Passion is a hard thing to conceal.

Security

Your home is where you make your living.

The distance one should keep from a evil man cannot be
measured.

Young Benin King

Self-Esteem

Without being overconfident, believe in yourself.

It's always better to be better than you think you can be.

Self-Defense

There may come a time when you must do what you must do.

Self-Examination

Before mending your neighbor's fence, look to your own.

If you always tell the truth, you don't need a good memory.

Self-Knowledge

Wisdom from above and within is always peaceful.

Listen to the wind and hear the voices of your life.

Service

Heal thyself, then heal others.

Sex

A warrior wants sex after violence.

The last thing civilized by man will be woman.

Sex and marriage go together.

Shame

A bad daughter gives a bad name to her father.

Size

A lion can drink much, but the elephant drinks more.

When building the pyramids, the Egyptians measured
twice and cut once.

Skepticism

In all times, in all places, the truth is beautiful.

Soul

A soul gets caught up in a love and is taught a whole
new rhythm.

Hearts and souls are colorless.

Speaking

One must listen more and talk less.

Speculation

If there were no lions in the jungle,
the leopard would be a great cat.

A man who does not mend his clothes will soon
have no clothes.

Although the berry tree is large, who knows how big its
yield will be.

You will be remembered if you do one thing superbly
well.

When you walk like your father, you learn how to avoid
pitfalls.

Strength

From your inner strength, somehow, choose the road
to heaven, or accept the road to hell.

In war, strategy is better than strength.

Stubbornness

Mothers-in-law hear only what they want to hear.

Heaven let it be too late.

Success

People who work together in one accord share eminent
success together.

If your ship stayed afloat, the storm was not important.

Sun

Without the sun, the moon would be a dark circle.

Our Father the Sun and Mother the Moon drew breath
from the
morning stars and we became alive.

Support

If no family member heeds your call, go forth alone.

Sympathy

Sorrow is like a treasure, shown only to a few close friends.

When a friend hurts her, a woman runs to her husband.

Talk

When the ear of understanding opens,
the words of wisdom speak.

African talk will revive conversation when conversation lags.

African talk is the daughter of truth and the son of love.

African talk and nature are related.

A cutting word is worse than a cutting bow string. A cut may heal, but a cutting word will never heal.

If you have nothing to say, never say it out loud.

Ajuba Drummer

Temptation

A sterilized woman can act as sexual as a sexual man.

Thankfulness

A one-eyed man only thanks God when he sees a
totally blind man.

I knew you before you were born.

Masquerade Celebration

Thought

Think slowly, but act quickly.

Bad thoughts inflame the mind as a wound
inflames the finger.

The last thing civilized by man will be woman.

The African experience is three dimensional: mental,
physical, and spiritual.

Why are there no pictures of camels on the pyramid
walls?

Time is the universal instructor.

Pharaoh threw a written message into the Nile to order
it to rise.

Most of the things we worry about never happen.

The rewards of life are children.

The heart can be broken by thoughts.

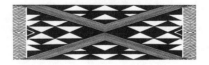

Masi mother and children

Truth

If you do what you should not do, you must bear what
you
cannot bear.

Truth is like gold—keep it locked up and you will find it
exactly as you first put it away.

The sweetest strawberry will not sweeten dry old bread.

A woman should never hide the father from the child.

A banana never bears a lime.

People fail to remember families are forever.

A thief is always under suspicion.

A smart enemy is better than an ignorant friend.

The night has ears, flies have ears, even fish have ears.

The lion who arrives early gets good drinking water, the
lion
who arrives late drinks mud.

The earth is forever shut from the heaven's roof.

The end of a cow is beef; the end of a lie is grief.

When a large, old tree falls, it kills a young one.

A tune is never finished if the drum is borrowed.

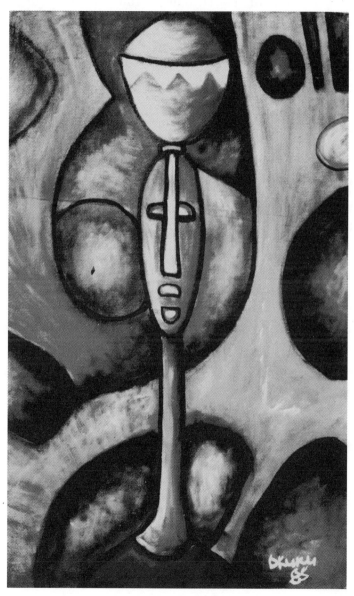

The Offering

When you hear the truth about injustice, it always sounds outrageous.

A man cannot count on riches.

One thousand truths are spoiled by one falsehood.

Everything has a beginning and an end.

The story of the Avatar (Christ) is true.

In the desert, you must learn to eat time.

Unfruitful

A woman without a good man is like a flower without seeds.

Unity

When women band together, they outlive men.

Lasour Ibibio

Universe

In the sunset we see all the vast colors, where the day
joins
past eternities.

Night by night we look right through the heavens
above and see God's roof.

Of all the responsibilities the sun has in the universe,
as if it
had nothing more to do, it ripens fruit.

The universal sign for earth is
the cross.
Any upheaval on earth is forewarned by the heavens.

Stars are like God's teeth, they sparkle like the
underbelly of a fish.

Virtue

Having wealth is not as good as having virtue.

Walking

Have a stick in your hand when snakes are at your feet.

When walking up the mountain lead with your good leg.
When walking down lead with your bad leg.

Benin Warriors

War

War is the most personal impersonal of feelings.

Man is obsessed with re-fighting old wars.

Wars are won by tactical superiority.

Early wars were won by the slaves.

To an old warrior, the outbreak of war is a gift
from the war God.

A nation of many races is hard to defeat.

Warning

Death never sounds a trumpet.

Death does not respect beauty.

Wife

Love's alright and things are changing.

Let love be genuine.

Wife, God will not change marriage.

Lasour Ekpo

Wisdom

We all begin as fools, through experience we become wise.

A wise man reconciles difficulties by knowing African talk.

Step aside and let rats shoot arrows at each other.

A wise man's heart lies quiet, like still water.

He who upsets a thing should know how to rearrange it.

It is not what you do, it's what you don't do. It is not what
you say, it's what you don't say.

The baby jackal gets the best of both worlds, it is educated
by both the mother and the father.

The fool killer is alive and busy.

The easiest form of mental activity is criticism, the toughest is creativity.

Go in peace.

South African Dancers

Wit

An old man who runs alone cannot be outrun
by a younger man.

Woman

All women are born with two traps—one for babies
and one for men.

God has made a flower for every woman.

A man and woman who love each other, think about
each
other on two occasions. Day and night.

All women are one kind of a flower.

Where there is no male influence, the offspring suffers.

God will not change marriage.

Masi Mothers Working

Words

If foul words from your mouth turned into a knife, it
would cut off your lips.

Good words are worth much, but cost you nothing.

Wrong

It is wrong not to go in peace.

Artist Biography:
Prince Emmanuel Okuku

Okuku was born to the Chief of Ikot Antia in the State of Akwa Ibom, Nigeria in 1942. He was educated at the Commercial Academy in Uyo. His talent was manifested very early in life. By the age of seven, he was already doing murals on the walls of his father's compound, with colored chalk and charcoal. By nine, his teachers had him doing sketches on the school wall.

After schooling Okuku moved to Lagos. His work soon caught the attention of the famous artist Demakos, who studied under Picasso. Demakos was so impressed by Okuku that he took him to Brazaville, Zaire where he was carefully coached for five years. He returned to Nigeria in 1963 and immediately set up his own studio.

Okuku likens his work to infinite road maps—at any point of contact, the eyes move over the entire painting. He refers to this as a continuous movement, with no beginning and no end. His favorite illusion is hiding faces inside the spaces of the mosaic canvas. Okuku created a striking variety of paintings in which tribal rituals and music, musical instruments and mask form integral visual elements and themes. They vary considerably, all along stylized figurations with a deep sense of Africanness.

Okuku's patrons are spread across three continents, from the government statehouse in Calabar, Nigeria, the

United Kingdom, Italy, Germany, Switzerland, Spain, Sweden, Denmark, France, Finland, Greece, and the United States of America.

Grateful acknowledgment to Mrs. Lizabeth Okuku Bombata, sister of Okuku and owner of Designs by Lizzie, Richmond Heights, Ohio, for permission to use Okuku's pictures.

—Carlos Vintes Pender
Author, *African Talk*